This amazingly [...] success is what [...] were waiting for. In its direct and clear style it takes you to the root of the problems of inequality in our society and provides the guidelines for our children to accomplish great things in the future. A must read!

—Justo G. Herrera
Parent, educator, writer, and entrepreneur, founder of Marisstella Oneworld Marketing LLC, coffeeandyou.com, and eaglesreborn.com.

This is an honest, timely, and effective tool for parents and families as they attempt to raise their children in a challenging and changing world.

—Jim Ford
Principal, St Cecilia School St. Louis.

This book provides informative, straight-forward, hands on strategies for students of different ages to assist them in choosing as well as following through on their interests, career decisions, and daily practices that promote success and positive futures.

—Lisa D. Smith
Former St. Louis Public Schools elementary teacher presently working as curriculum and activities coordinator for T.R.O.U.T.S. (Teens Reaching Out-Up Towards Success).

FORWARD MARCH to PROFESSIONALISM

FORWARD MARCH to PROFESSIONALISM

Starting Early to Help Latino American Children Develop a Vision of Their Dream Careers

CAJETAN NGOZIKA IHEWULEZI

TATE PUBLISHING & *Enterprises*

Published by Tate Publishing & Enterprises, LLC
127 E. Trade Center Terrace | Mustang, Oklahoma 73064 USA
1.888.361.9473 | www.tatepublishing.com

Tate Publishing is committed to excellence in the publishing industry. The company reflects the philosophy established by the founders, based on Psalm 68:11,
"The Lord gave the word and great was the company of those who published it."

Book design copyright © 2009 by Tate Publishing, LLC. All rights reserved.
Cover design by Lance Waldrop
Interior design by Stefanie Rooney

Published in the United States of America

ISBN: 978-1-60799-025-3
1. Self-Help, Time Management
2. Self-Help, Personal Growth, General
09.04.20

Dedicated to my little Latino
friends across the country

ACKNOWLEDGEMENT

I am thankful to the following for their advice, expertise, and support in the production of this book. Rev. Gary Meier, Rev. Truman, Rev. William Vatterott, Sr. Pat Chaffee, Sr. Pat Bober CSJ, Sr. Gail Trippett CSJ, Ms. Allison Gray, Mr. Jim Ford, Mr. Justo G. Herrera, Lisa Smith, Edgar Ramirez, Heather Sieve, and Nilsa S. Barreras.

I thank the many Latino children whose pictures are featured in this book. I also thank their parents for granting me the permission to use the pictures of their children.

Finally, I am thankful to the Principal, the staff, and students of St Cecilia School and Academy in South St. Louis for their contributions to the writing of this book.

TABLE OF CONTENTS

A MESSAGE TO LATINO AMERICAN PARENTS AND OTHERS WHO TAKE CARE OF LATINO YOUTH

As a pastor who has worked in a Latino church and youth camp for many years, my encounters with our Latino youth in this country make me feel that many of them (as do the youths of every race), still need additional motivation and guidance to be more interested in education and in some professional careers. It is not that some of our youth are not having adequate guidance from their parents, but with the jails "still packed full with unusually high percentage of Blacks and Hispanics,"[1] and due to other reasons that cause absence of fathers in their families, many of them may not be getting enough direction and motivation that should be provided by both parents. "Too many absent fathers leave too many poor and minority children in families headed by single mothers struggling financially and straining to hold their households together."[2]

A great number of Latino parents work long tiresome hours with the hopes of providing for their children the social and financial environment for them to succeed. Yet, the meager pay-checks they bring home are not enough to afford the better schools and better living and health environment some other groups enjoy. Perhaps Latino parents tell their children (many of them first generation Americans) of their proud heritage, a new people born out of conquest and suffering, daring and adaptation, a heritage that ruled kingdoms and formed modern nations, but the children look at their own struggling parents and sometimes find it difficult to see the greatness they hear about.

So how do we provide supportive motivation to our Latino youth to be more interested in their education and to become professionals, to be able to change the economic and social status of their families? The best way is to start early in helping them plan their lives and focus their attention more on what their *dream career*, or purpose in life is, and to guide them in applying the type of discipline required to achieve it. Every Latino parent would like his or her children to be better than he or she is. Because of the Latino parents' many poorly rewarded hours of work in a certain low paying non-professional jobs, he or she would like his sons and daughters in the future to

become well educated and successful professionals in different fields of life.

This book however, is written to speak directly
to all Latino children within the ages of seven
and eleven, as a father or mother speaks to his
or her children, about starting early and having
a vision of what could be their *dream career* and
developing the discipline that would help them
achieve their dreams. It is to act as a guide to a
planned life, with or without the motivation of
their parents.

Chapter one of this book helps them to develop
the much required self-confidence (self-esteem)
and to be happy with who they are, not only as
human beings, but also as Latino youth with a
mission to contribute to our society. It also helps
them to know their connection with God and
their equality with every other human being—
irrespective of sex, race, color, and age. It makes
known to them the place of God in their future
careers and how God has blessed them with talents and gifts. It encourages them to start having
a vision of what their dream career or profession
is going to be from the early age of seven.

Chapter two looks into what goes on in their
families, offering the type of discipline needed,

beginning at home, which they can apply even before going to school. It attempts to let them know the basic responsibilities of home and suggests basic time management skills needed even when their parents may or may not be there to tell them every thing to do and when to do them.

Chapter three discusses the importance of education in their lives, and how they can become prominent Americans and professionals, by taking their education seriously. This chapter also includes a detailed look of what happens from entering the school bus in the morning to what happens at the end of the school day.

Finally, each chapter of this book ends with a prayer to help them develop a consciousness that, apart from education and working hard, they also need to recognize that all successes come from the hands of God. They cannot do without God.

The best way to help our youth stay out of trouble is to start early to help them plan their lives and focus their attention more on what is their *dream* or purpose in life and to guide them in applying the type of discipline required to achieve it. If this is effectively done in every Latino family, I believe that poverty will be drastically reduced in Latino communities, and less of our children will be in prison and murdered along the streets in gang related violence.

The next book is a detailed guide to self discipline, educational success, professionalism, and leadership for Latino American teenagers.

CHAPTER ONE

YOU AND YOUR DREAMS

My beloved children, if somebody comes to you and asks you this question; "Who are you?" What will you say about yourself? Whatever you say, I know already that you have a beautiful name or beautiful names given to you by your parents. You are members of your families. You are also true citizens of America. Above all, you are children of God.

As a member of your family, you are loved by your parents. Your brothers and sisters and your friends also love you. You have some rights like every other member of your family, and so you should be treated well like others in your family.

As a citizen of America, you have rights just like all other Americans. You should also be treated equal to other Americans irrespective of sex, race, color, and age.

You are children of God because you were created by God in his image and likeness (Gen 1:27). This is why you are beautiful, handsome, sweet, lovable, and special.

A good example of a beautiful Latino creation of God

It does not matter if you are a boy or a girl. It does not matter if you are tall or short, skinny or big. Your sex, age, and the color of your skin may be different; but the image of God in you is not different from the image of God in your friends whom you meet at school, at the park and in the shopping malls. The image of God in you is the first thing and the most important quality that makes you really who you are. So you are equal to your friends and other human beings. You should therefore, feel good about yourself. The reason why God created you in his image and likeness is because He loves you and wants you to be successful.

Some Latino children play with their friends at school.

You Are Made for a Purpose

After creating us, God not only blessed us to be fruitful; he also asked us to work hard so as to increase and multiply, to fill the earth and to subdue it (Gen.1:28). Since God wants you to be fruitful, he wants you to take part in the work of creation and in making the world more beautiful.

Apart from being a child of God, a member of your family and a citizen of America, God has not finished with you. You still need other qualities that will add up to make you who you are as you grow older. God wants you to grow and develop and achieve great things because he created you for a purpose. To achieve the purpose for which he created you, God has blessed you with talents, intelligence, and wisdom. These gifts make you special. Your friends are also special in their own ways and have also been blessed with gifts.

Use Your Talents and Intelligence to Become Great

When God created you, like every one else, you did not take part in what God did for you. Yet the same time, God wants you, as a human being, to take part in doing something that will make you **become** great in the future.

So God wants you to be somebody important, and to help in making your family, your country, and the world better. You are therefore expected to use your talents wisely to achieve great things in the future.

Talents are those things you take joy in doing and that you can do very well. Everyone has his or her own talents or gifts. For example, you may be good in singing or in drawing beautiful pictures or playing the piano or playing football or soccer. It is your responsibility to find out the talent God has given to you and try to develop it.

Christian Gonzalez, 9, in fourth grade, enjoys developing his talent of playing the guitar. Though he dreams of becoming a pilot, he also loves playing his guitar for fun.

Since God made you for a purpose, he also wants you to develop a career or a profession from the talent and intelligence he has given you. Your career or your profession is the job you are going to be doing in the future like your dads and moms. The words career and profession mean almost the same thing. So we shall use them interchangeably in this book.

Through your career or profession, you will earn money every month to maintain yourself and your future family when you become adults. You can be a medical doctor, pharmacist, an engineer, an attorney, a priest, an architect, a policeman, a soldier, and so on. There are other professions or careers; I am just mentioning a few. Your career can be seen as the purpose for which God created you. Having a career is an opportunity for you to serve God and humanity and your opportunity to contribute to making the world a better place to live.

Whatever you want to be in the future depends on what you are interested in doing or what you are talented in. For example, if you like to build and fix things with your hands, you can be a good engineer, construction worker, carpenter, electrician, or plumber. If you like to take care of people who are sick, you can be a good medical doctor or nurse. If you like talking to people, you can be a good broadcaster, politician, news reporter, and social worker. If you like to solve problems with numbers, you can be a good math teacher, a banker or an accountant.

Tell Us What You Want To Be

Let me tell you how I became what I am now. Maybe this will help you to start thinking about what you want to be. When I was young like you, I remember my father and my mother asking me to tell them what I wanted to be. They asked, "What are you going to be when you become an adult?" I answered, "I don't know because I am still a child."

My father told me, "You are ten years old and you are no longer a baby. At ten, you have reached the age of reasoning and you should start now to plan your life and think of how to spend your life. I do not want you to be a loser. Even if you will change your mind, you should start now to think about a career and we, your parents, shall guide you."

Yes, at age ten, eleven or twelve, it could be right to argue that it is a bit early to start thinking of what one is going to be as an adult. At the same time, "it's the perfect time to start making some important discoveries about who you are. What you like to do and what you do best. It's the ideal time to start thinking about what you want to do."[3] Some people even start earlier from the ages of seven, eight or nine to make some discoveries about themselves and about things they love doing very well.

My parents gave me time to think about how I was going to spend my life in future. After some time, my father called me again and asked me what I was going to be. I answered, "I am going to be a priest or a pastor in a church."

When I told them that I was going to be a priest, everyone in my family started calling me "little priest," or "little pastor." My mother then asked me, "Why do you want to be a priest?" I answered, "Because I like the behavior of the Irish priest in our church and I want to serve God like him and help people to feel good."

I was happy that I was going to have a good profession and that I was not going to live my life as a *loser*. A *loser* is someone who does not want to go to school and work hard to earn a living. I also did not want to live my life as someone who would depend on welfare while young and healthy.

When I told my friends that I wanted to be a priest, they also started calling me "little pastor" or "little priest." By calling me "little priest," I knew that I should start behaving well to make sure that I do not lose that name and to avoid disappointing those who were already calling me that name. I was ready to discipline myself to become a pastor. Even if I had changed my mind in future, at least I was aiming to be somebody important for myself, to my family and to my community.

So if I asked you the same question which my parents asked me, what would be your answer? If your parents have not asked you this question, I am now asking you to tell me what you are going to be. Are you going to be an attorney, a medical doctor, a nurse, an engineer, a priest, a pilot, a soldier or a news broadcaster? What else do you want to be? This is like asking you what your *dream career* is.

Since God created you for a purpose, you must give an answer and be ready to play your own part in achieving your dreams. No reasonable person will ever say that he or she wants to be a loser, or an armed robber, or a drug addict. God did not create you for such purposes. God did not create you or anyone to be a loser but to be a winner.

Look at these pictures below. Little Juan Herrera, seven, in second grade, is dreaming of becoming a lawyer or an attorney. He loves watching lawyers doing their job on television. Speaking with him, I saw how enthusiastic he was about becoming a lawyer. He is ready to undergo some disciplines at home, at school and in the wider American society to be able to achieve his dreams.

Little Juan Herrera, seven, in second grade, is already dreaming of becoming a lawyer to defend justice.

Little Jose Herrera, eight, in third grade, is dreaming of becoming a medical doctor. He visits children's hospitals and loves watching doctors take care of his fellow children. He was also once a patient and was happy when a female doctor talked to him in a very loving way. He told me that he loves the profession and would do every thing possible to be a doctor.

Little Jose Herrera, eight, in third grade,
is already dressed like a medical doctor
and dreams of becoming one.

How Do You Know What You Would Like To Be?

When my father and mother asked me to tell them what I wanted to be, it was not easy, but it made me start thinking about all the things I am interested in, my talents, and the things I enjoyed doing most. I thought about different careers or professions I liked. I also started thinking about people I liked and how they did their jobs. As I have already told you, I liked the Irish pastor in my parish and the job he was doing. I dreamed of being like him.

You must have an interest in any career you dream about. There may be certain people who influence you or who seem so happy in their job, you would like to do the same thing. These are the people we call *role models*. Your parents, uncles, and aunties may be your role models, and you may want to do what they are doing or become professionals like them. You may want to be a medical doctor, or an engineer, or an attorney because your father or mother is one. You may want to be a soldier, or a police officer, or a construction worker, or pharmacist because your uncle or your auntie is one.

In the picture below, little Teresita Carillo, eleven, is dreaming of becoming a pharmacist like her auntie. She loves her auntie's profession and would like to be like her.

Little Teresita Carrillo, eleven, in sixth grade is already dreaming of becoming a pharmacist like her auntie.

If your parents and other relations are not professionals in their jobs, you may need other role models. Even your parents would wish that you aim higher than them and do better than them. If they are not professionals, they would like you to be one. If your parents are not your role models in the profession you dream about, family friends and other people can also be your role models.

In the picture below, little Josemaria, seven, in second grade, is dreaming of becoming a registered nurse (RN) like one of his father's family friends. He also visits children's hospitals and watches male nurses doing their jobs and would like to be like to follow their footsteps.

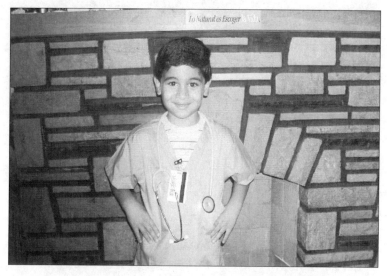

Little Josemaria, seven in second grade dreams of becoming a registered nurse like his father's family friend. He also likes watching male nurses working in children's hospitals.

You Can Also Do It

When you see role models like scientists, medical doctors, or pharmacists, or engineers, or pilots, or attorneys, or pastors, or bankers, or farmers, you may ask yourself a question, "Can I do it?" I am telling you now, you can also do it. Just tell yourself that you can. Why is it that I am telling you that you can also do it? The reason is that God created your *role models* with some talents, intelligence, and wisdom. Your role models used these gifts from God and worked so hard in their education and in other areas to improve on them and so became what they are.

God has also given you enough intelligence and wants you to use them wisely to grow, develop, and to be what you want to be. If your *role models* worked hard to succeed, you can also work hard to succeed like them. Apart from working hard in your education and training, you must also continue to be a child of God and be close to God in prayers.

Prayer of a Latino Child for God's Guidance

Dear God I thank you for making me who I am. Thank you for loving me and for making me in your image and likeness. Thank you for giving me talents to work for you and to work for humanity. As a growing child Lord, I need your help and your Spirit to direct me on what to do. Help me to be wise to plan my life and to choose a career you have prepared for me in life.

When I am feeling unloved, help me to

know how much you love me. When I am lonely, help me to know how close you are to me. When I am afraid, make me be strong. When I am in danger, protect me. When people look down on me, help me to work hard and prove to them what I can achieve. When I am lazy, give me the strength to work hard. When I am ignorant, make me wise. When I am oppressed, be my defender, my rock, and my source of justice.

Help me to be law-abiding and obedient to you, to my parents and to my community. I know that without you, I can do nothing. With you Lord everything is possible for me. Help me to do my best in achieving my dreams. Amen.

He is praying for God's guidance. Apart from taking his education seriously, he knows that prayer is part of the effort he should make in order to succeed in life. With God by your side, you can overcome all obstacles in achieving your dream career.

After saying this prayer, I want you to feel the presence of God around you, the love of God in your heart, and the Spirit of God directing you on the right things to do wherever you find yourself. This prayer has to be said occasionally as you pursue your dream career. You could add other prayers your pastor taught you in your church or religion.

Homework and Questions

- How do you feel about yourself or what can you say about yourself? Write down five things you like about yourself as God made you.

- What makes you feel equal to your friends and to other human beings?

  As a member of your family.

  As a citizen of your country.

  As a child of God.

- Why did God create you in his image and likeness?

- What are your talents, or things you enjoy doing most? You may not be good in doing everything. Write down about three things you do very well.

- What is your *dream career,* or what would you like to be in future? Write it down on a sheet of paper and show it to your parents and to your friends. .

- Why do you want to be what you are dreaming to be?

- Do you have a *role model?* Who is the person and why is he or she your **role** *model?* What is the profession of your role model?

- Do you believe that you can do what other people have done or what your *role model* has done? If yes, write down on a sheet of paper why you feel that you can do it.

- Who is a *loser?* Did God create you to be a *loser?* If the answer is no, mention the gifts God has given to you and what you should do with them to avoid becoming a *loser* in future.

- Do you remember to pray to God to guide you to be successful in achieving your *dream career?*

CHAPTER TWO

HOME DISCIPLINE AND YOUR FUTURE CAREER

My beloved children, to be a professional, you will need to start early to plan your life and to accept some disciplines at home, at school and in society. Your home is the first place where you will start preparing yourself for whatever you want to be in future. This means you must start being good or disciplined from your home. Being disciplined from home involves obeying the simple rules which your parents have made.

When you start being good and behaving well by obeying family rules, your family members may start respecting you and start calling you the name of whatever you want to be. As I told you, when I told my parents that I wanted to become a pastor, I started being good and behaving well like a good pastor. My brothers and sisters started calling me "little pastor" because of my good behaviors at home. If you want to be a medical doctor, a lawyer, a business person, or any other thing you want to be, tell your family and start behaving well, they may also start calling you little doctor, little lawyer, little business person or little whatever you want to be.

Whether they call you such names or not, your parents and brothers and sisters will expect you to start acting in responsible ways. Before I tell you about some family rules that could guide you to start behaving well like a disciplined child, let us first talk about the type of relationship that should exist in your home between you and other members of your family.

You must love, respect, and obey your parents. This is the root of your success in whatever career you dream about. You must also love and respect your siblings and every human being you meet.

Respect and Obey Your Parents

Your parents are the first people that want you to become successful in life and are generally the first to help you know what you should do and what you should not do in order to achieve your dreams. As I already told you, even if your parents are not professionals, they more than likely want you to do as well as, if not better than them; hoping for better opportunities than they have had.

Because your parents are generally the first to

wish you well, you must obey and respect them. No good parent or parents will ever want their children to do something wrong. I know you have good parents and you should be loyal to them. When obedience and respect start from home, you will find it easier to apply the same respect and obedience at school with your teachers at the different levels of your education. This is the root to your success.

Apart from your parents, you should also respect and consider your brothers and sisters and other members of your family. Here are some sample rules that may guide you to be more disciplined at home.

Guiding Rules about Relating with Other Members of Your Family

- Respect, love, and obey your parents.
- Respect, love and consider your siblings or brothers and sisters.
- Share with your brothers and sisters and treat them as you would like them treat you.
- Be polite and do not be rude in talking to or in dealing with others in your family.

- Always use these words when required: "thank you," "please," and "I am sorry."

- Do not fight.

- Do not steal.

- Do not tell anyone lies.

- Do not use bad language or call your siblings bad names.

- Instead of fighting, report to your parents when someone hurts you in the house or at school.

The Discipline of General House Cleanliness

To be a professional also involves keeping your environment clean. It is more difficult to succeed in any profession if your environment is always dirty. If your office is always dirty, people will not like to come in. The first place where you learn how to keep your office clean is at your home. Here are some sample rules that will guide you to keep your home and future office clean.

Guiding Rules about Keeping the House Clean

- Do not leave dirty dishes and food items on the floor or lying around.

- Do not drop your clothes, shoes, caps, and your books on the floor

- Clean up your own mess anywhere in the house.

- Flush the toilet after using it.

- Remember to do your chores and do them well at the proper time.

- Do no argue or fight with your parents when they tell you to do your chores.

Personal Cleanliness and Your Career

To be a professional also means that you have to be presentable to your clients. For example, if a medical doctor or an attorney is dirty and smelly, no one likes to come close to him or her. No matter what you want to be, you should start now to be clean and dress well.

If you dress rough or raggedy and keep your hair bushy, people will not take you seriously. Even at school, if you do not look clean, your friends will not like to sit with you on the school bus and in the classroom. Personal cleanliness is also good for your health. If you are dirty, you can get sick easily. When you fall sick, you will miss your lessons at school and that can affect your future career. Here are some sample rules that can help you to be neat as you are supposed to be when you become a professional.

Guiding Rules about Cleaning and Keeping Yourself Clean

- Brush your teeth when you wake up in the morning.

- Wash your hands and clean yourself well after using the toilet.

- Take a shower at least once every day. If there is time in the morning, do it when you wake from sleep or do it in the evening or before going to bed. Taking your shower twice a day, morning and evening is very good.

- Keep your clothes, shoes, and socks clean.

- Do not drop your clothes, shoes, and socks on the floor.

- Drop your dirty clothes, underwear, and socks inside a hamper or laundry bag.

- Keep your sleeping areas neat and tidy.

- Maintain your hair and do not allow it to be bushy.

To be a professional, you must learn from home how to keep yourself clean and healthy. The environment where you live and do your studies should also be clean.

Eating Habit, Table Manners, and Your Career

To be a professional also involves controlling your eating habits so that you can move sharply and quickly. To be overweight is not good for anyone.

Always listen to your parents when they warn you not to eat junk food or take dangerous drugs and alcohol at your age.

The home is also where you learn some table etiquette. If you are a doctor, or a nurse, or a banker, or a pastor, and you go to a party with your friends and they discover that you have no table manners, it does not make a good impression. Here are some sample rules that will also help you.

Guiding Rules about Eating in the House and Table Manners

- Come to eat with others at the proper time when food is ready.

- Wash your hands, and if possible your face, and free yourself of any tight clothes you are wearing.

- Observe simple table manners like considering others when taking your food, not talking when you have food in your mouth, closing your mouth while chewing, taking small bites, and not playing with your food.

- Take your dishes to where they should be

washed or place them in dishwasher if there is one and clean crumbs.

- Do not take drugs that are not prescribed.

Doing Your Studies and Your Homework

You cannot be a professional if you are failing in your school work. Doing your studies at home and spending some time to do your homework helps you to get better grades and to succeed. Playing away your time and spending your whole time watching television after school will not help you.

How do you feel when you get poor grades? I do not expect you to be happy when your classmates are making better grades. It is not that God did not give you intelligence and wisdom as others. As I have already told you, God has given you enough intelligence and wisdom to succeed in any thing you want to be. You only need to work hard in everything you are doing, especially in your education.

Guiding Rules about Doing Your Studies at Home

- Do your homework after school if possible everyday and hand it to your teachers at the proper time.

- Spend enough time everyday, at least one hour on your studies, either doing your homework or reading old lessons or preparing for new lessons ahead of the teacher. Spend at least seven to eight hours on your studies every week.

- Making arrangement to call your teacher on the phone to help you if you are finding something difficult while reading or doing your homework.

- If your teacher is not available, call any of your school friends who can help you clear your confusion

You cannot be a professional without taking your studies seriously. Spend enough time everyday, at least one hour on your studies, either doing your homework or reading old lessons or preparing for new lessons ahead of the teacher. Spend at least seven to eight hours on your studies every week.

Watching Television, Playing Video Games, and Achieving Your Dream Career

How many hours do you spend watching television and playing video games everyday? If you watch television or play video games for too many hours and forget your studies and other home activities, you may find it difficult to achieve your dream career. You will not be able to make good grades at school if you do not spend enough time on your studies. You must be in control of how much television you watch. There must be scheduled time for everything, including watching television and playing video games.

When watching television, watch channels that help you develop more interest in your dream profession. For example, some channels like Discovery, National Geographic, as well as historical and scientific channels can help you more.

Watching television or playing video games should not take the place of your studies. Watch television only when you have finished your chores and homework. There should be control on how much time you spend on watching television and playing video games.

Guiding Rules about Watching Television

- Know when to turn the television on.

- Watch television only when you have finished your chores and homework. You can use it for relaxation after dinner.

- If there is a special program, get your parents' permission to watch it.

- While watching television, look for role models that will encourage you to work hard to achieve your dream career.

- Do not watch programs not properly noted for your age.

- Watch channels related to your career and your educational dreams like discovery, health, law, geographic, history, and religion.

- Know when to turn off the television and go to bed.

Spending Time on Your Hobbies

What are your hobbies or things you like doing for leisure? You may be talented or you may be interested in playing soccer, basketball, singing, playing the piano, painting, writing stories, keeping pet animals or other things. These may be hobbies, at the same time; you can develop any of your hobbies into a profession or a career in future.

Apart from spending time on your studies at home, you may need to spend some time practicing your piano skills, basketball skills, soccer skill or guitar skills—whatever you are interested in doing. You may not have enough time during the week, but you may have more time on the weekends.

I encourage you if at all possible to spend some time on these skills every day, no matter how small. Sometimes it is harder to maintain your skill if you only practice on weekends. You may forget the skills you have already learned. Here are some sample guiding rules.

Guiding Rules about Doing Your Hobbies

- Know your hobby or hobbies and when to do them.
- Spend at least ten to twenty minutes everyday to re-touch the skills after school.

- Spend more time on them during the weekends.

- Appeal to your parents to buy the materials needed for your hobbies (To make your parents be more interested in buying materials for your hobbies, you must be good children, respecting and obeying your parents).

- Appeal to your parents to hire special teachers to coach you on the skills if they can afford it.

She enjoys playing her musical instrument everyday after doing her chores and her studies or home work. She spends at least ten to twenty minutes everyday on the skills. Though she dreams of becoming an accountant, she also loves playing her musical instrument as a hobby.

Leisure Activities

You cannot be a good professional if you are not physically fit. My teacher used to tell me when I was ten, "all work without play makes Jack a dull boy." You need exercise to keep fit. I know that many of you do enough leisure play or exercises during break times at school. However, your parents can also allow you to take a walk or go out with friends to the park in the evenings.

Guiding Rules about Leisure Activities

- Go out for leisure activities (swimming, basketball, baseball, and soccer) when possible, especially when you have finished your homework and during the weekends when your parents allow you.

- Play safe and do not enter into trouble with your friends.

- Know when to stop leisure activities and go home to carry out other activities.

To be a professional, you need to be physically fit.
Taking part in physical exercises will help you a lot.

Going to Bed and Waking Up

It is part of home discipline to go to bed on time so that you can wake up on time. If you go to bed late, you will not only wake up late, you will also be late for school and sleep in class. When you sleep in class, you will miss and not understand what the teacher is saying, causing you to fail your tests.

When you keep failing your tests, you may not qualify to study for your dream profession. So you will need to keep to your bedtime. If your parents tell you to go to bed by eight p.m., or at any time they deem fit for you, do not keep watching the television or playing around and arguing with them. A disciplined child does not argue with his or her parents when told to do the right thing.

Guiding Rules about Going to Bed and Waking up

- Keep your bed time. This should be early enough so that you will be able to wake up early.

- Keep to your wake up time. This should be early enough so that you will be prepared for school.

- Do not fight with your parents when they try to wake you up.

- Use an alarm clock to help you wake up on time.

- Brush your teeth and wash your face, if possible take your shower and prepare for school or other activities.

- It is also advisable to pray before going to bed to ask God to protect you while you sleep and to pray when you wake up from sleep to thank God for making you wake up fine. Here are sample prayers.

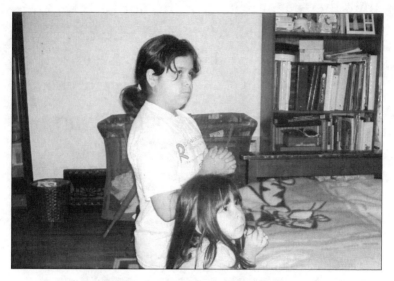

*Before going to bed, it is important to ask
God to protect you while you sleep.*

Prayer before Going to Bed

*Dear God I thank you for protecting me in
all I did today. Now I am about to go to bed,
protect me in body and in spirit while I sleep.
Protect also my parents, my brothers and sisters, and my friends as they sleep. May your
spirit be with us to make us feel your presence,
love, and care. May we wake up tomorrow in
peace and in healthy conditions to continue
our normal daily activities. Amen.*

When you wake up from sleep in the morning, it is also important to thank God for protecting you.

Prayer after waking from Sleep

Dear God I thank you so much for granting me a peaceful sleep over the night. Thank you also for helping me to wake up healthy enough to start a new day. Help me in all I will do today to act correctly as expected and according to your will. Amen.

You can say other prayers your parents or pastor taught you in your church.

Getting Ready for School in the Morning

Going to school has to be prepared for and should be taken seriously. You cannot start looking for your books and looking for your shoes when you should be at the bus stop waiting to get on the school bus. This can make you late. When you are late to school, you distract everyone in class when the lesson is going on. You will also miss what was taught before you came in, and this can affect your grades.

Guiding Rules about Getting Ready for School

- Before going to bed, get your school bag ready with the right books and materials needed inside.

- Get your school clothes ready. Place them where you can find them easily in the morning.

- Do not wake up late.

- Wash up properly to be neat and to avoid being smelly at school.

- Wait for the school bus early and do not misbehave inside the school bus

- Do not look for trouble or hurt any of your friends inside the school bus.

- Do not fight, but report to the bus driver if anyone hurts you in any way. If the bus driver does not help you, report to your teacher or to the principal. If the teacher or the principal does not help you, report to your parents, especially if the person keeps bothering you.

The Rules Above Are To Help You

These rules may look difficult or they may seem simple, but keeping them will help you to be disciplined and organized. These rules are made by your parents or guardians to help you and not just to make things difficult for you. Not obeying these rules may attract some punishment. Obeying them will make you live in peace with your family members and help you to achieve your dreams.

Having a Week Day Schedule or Time Table and Your Dream Career

Having a schedule or a list of activities and the time they should be carried out during the weekdays or weekends is very important. No one likes to be regulated. However, having a schedule helps you to learn how to be more organized. It can also help you in your future careers because it is very hard if not impossible to achieve success in any career without the discipline of keeping to time and having a plan of what to do each day.

Below is a sample schedule I have drawn up for you. Your parents or guardians may have something better than this. In case your parent or parents are not able to draw up a schedule to help you organize your day, this can be of help.

Suggested Weekday Schedule

6:00 a.m.	Rise out of bed and take a couple of minutes to thank God for the new day (prayer after waking from sleep).
6:15 a.m.	Go into the bathroom and wash up. Wash your face, brush your teeth, and if possible, take a shower.
6:30 a.m.	Get dressed and check to make sure that your schoolbag and other personal and school items are ready.

6:45 a.m.	Have breakfast if possible, or you may have it at school depending on the practice of your school district. This is the most important meal of your day. Your body needs nourishment to function well.
7:00 a.m.	At this time, you'll be on your way to school, either catching a bus or being driven to school. During this time you should prepare yourself mentally to succeed in your classes. Decide again today that you are going to be the best that you can be, as a student, as a classmate, and as a citizen.

3:00 p.m. to 4:00 p.m.	You are returning home. Make a mental or visual review of all your assignments, projects, and topics of study for that afternoon and evening. (Some schools give students an assignment book. Students should fill in their assignment book each day before they leave school. Parents, look at the assignment book with their child before and after homework time. Assignment books can also be used for exchanging notes between the teachers and he parents).
4:00 p.m. to 4.30 p.m.	Free time to relax and take your snacks and to get prepared to do your chores and homework

4.30 p.m. to 5.30 p.m.	Do your house chores. These are tasks that you do with love as a valuable member of your family: it may be dusting the furniture, taking out the trash, washing some dishes, picking up toys, running an errand to the store, feeding the pets, etc.
5.30 p.m. to 6.30 p.m.	Begin to do all your school work. Start with what may seem more difficult to do. Try to work in a quite area in the house. Finish everything.
6.30 p.m. to 7.30 p.m.	This time should be family dinner time. Help your parent or parents to prepare the meals if possible or to set the table for meal. Gather around the table, and after thanking God for that delicious meal, eat and enjoy listening to everyone's stories of thc day, and telling one or two of your own.

CAJETAN NGOZIKA IHEWULEZI

7.30 p.m. to 8.30p.m.	During this approximate time relax and enjoy doing something you really like: watch a little TV with other family members, practice your talent (drawing, playing a musical instrument, singing, dancing), play a board game, read a fun book, listen to some music, and use the computer if needed.
8.30 p.m. to 8.45 p.m.	Take a quick shower. Prepare your clothing for the next day. Get your book bag ready. Bid the whole family good night. Receive your parents' blessings with veneration. Say your prayer of thanks (prayer before going to sleep).

If there are some other activities which are not put in this schedule, you can fix them where they are more comfortable for you.

Suggested Saturday Schedule or Time Table

8:00 a.m.	Rise out of bed and take a couple of minutes to thank God for the new day (prayer after waking from sleep).
8:15 a.m. to 8:30 a.m.	Go into the bathroom and wash up. Wash your face, brush your teeth, and if possible take a fast shower.
8:30 a.m. to 9:30 a.m.	Plan your day, eat breakfast and get ready to do your Saturday chores.
9:30 am to 11:30 a.m.	Do your weekend house chores. You have more time to do a more general cleaning of your house: it may involve doing your laundry, vacuuming the rooms, mowing the lawn outside the house, dusting the furniture, taking out the trash, washing some dishes, picking up toys, running an errand to the store or helping your parents to do shopping, feeding the pets, etc.

11:30 a.m. to 12:30 p.m.	Help your parents to prepare for lunch.
12:30 p.m. to 1:30 p.m.	Take your lunch, relax and take some rest.
1:30 p.m. to 3:30 p.m.	Studies: Read ahead of your teacher and prepare new lessons so as to make good contribution in class next week.
3:30 p.m. to 4:30 p.m.	Spend some time on your hobbies or practice your talents (playing a musical instrument, drawing, painting, singing, dancing, play a board game, read a fun book, listen to some music, and use the computer if needed).
4:30 p.m. to 6:00 p.m.	Go out with friends for some games or for some sporting activities (basketball, soccer, baseball, swimming, athletics, and gymnastics).
6:00 p.m. to 6:30 p.m.	Take a quick shower after your exercises.

6:30 p.m. to 7:30 p.m.	This time should be family dinner time. Help your parent or parents to prepare the meals if possible or to set the table for meal. Gather around the table, and after thanking God for that delicious meal, eat and enjoy listening to everyone's stories of the day, and telling one or two of your own.
7.30 p.m. to 8.30p.m.	During this approximate time relax and enjoy watching a little TV with other family members. Tell more stories and listen to other members of the family tell theirs.
8.30 p.m. to 8.45 p.m.	Prepare your clothing for Sunday worship the next day. Bid the whole family good night. Receive your parents' blessings with veneration. Say your prayer of thanks (prayer before going to sleep).

Suggested Sunday Schedule or Time Table

8:00 a.m.	Rise out of bed and take a couple of minutes to thank God for the new day (prayer after waking from sleep).
8:15 a.m. to 8:30 a.m.	Go into the bathroom and wash up. Wash your face, brush your teeth, and if possible take a fast shower.
8.30 am to 9.30 p.m.	Help your parents to prepare for breakfast and eat your breakfast.
9.30 am to 1:30 p.m.	Be ready to go for Sunday services depending on when your church or synagogue holds its Sunday worship.
1:30 p.m. to 6:30 p.m.	Eat launch and enjoy other Sunday activities with your parents, friends, and relations (Going to the zoo and museums, going to movies, dancing, going to ball games at the stadium, relaxing, telling stories, playing games in the park, hobbies, working on the computer, studies, and finally taking your dinner as your parents direct.

6:30 p.m. to 7:30 p.m.	Take your shower. Spend some time on your hobbies, and other
7:30 p.m. to 8:30 p.m.	Relax with your family, watching television or telling stories.
8:30 p.m. to 8.45 p.m.	Prepare for school the next day; get your school bag with all the required books ready. Bid the whole family good night. Receive your parents' blessings with veneration. Say your prayer of thanks, (prayer before going to sleep).

Note: This time table like the ones above is just a suggestion. It is not final. Your parents and you can adjust and readjust it as it suits you best.

How do you spend Your Holidays and or Summer Vacation?

Holidays and summer vacation are days or periods of break time after months of active studies in the school environments. Summer vacation could last up to three months of not going to school daily as usual or following school regulations and instructions. It could be a tempting period for young people who may see this break as a period for over sleeping, not reading their books, spending too much time watching movies or television, playing video games, and even not doing their hobbies.

Though summer vacation is a break from active school work, it is not a period of wasting time on things that do not help you achieve your dreams. It is both a period for rest from active school work and a period for doing more things by yourself. This includes helping your parents do more chores in the house, reading your books, spending more time on your hobbies, doing some leisure activities, and getting school materials ready before school starts.

In some areas, summer vacation is better organized to help students utilize their time. There may be summer school which ends half day, summer camping, library visitations, computer lessons, sports instructions, music instructions, and other activities. In some areas, there may not be any such organized activities. Whether you have organized summer activities or not, it is good to know that you can achieve a lot that will help you in your future careers during this time. It is not wise to waist the whole period.

Here is a suggested time table of activities that can help you spend your vacation time better. This time table is not final. Unlike the other time tables above, I am not going to attach a definite time on each of the suggested activities. I am going to suggest a flexible time frame you and your parents or guardians can adjust and read just to suite you best. This time table can apply to summer vacation, Christmas and Easter breaks, and other holidays throughout the year.

Suggested Daily Summer Vacation Time Table of Activities

Waking up:	Try to rise out of bed in the morning at a time that will be suitable for you to attend summer school. Whether you have summer school or not, make sure you do not stay in bed after eight a.m. Staying in bed after eight a.m. may not be helpful. (Remember to say the prayer after waking from sleep).

Washing up:	Go into the bathroom and wash up. Wash your face, brush your teeth, and if possible take a fast shower. It should not take you more than thirty minutes to finish washing up.
Dress up:	Get dressed and be ready for the activities of the day. If you have summer school, check to make sure that your schoolbag and other personal and school items are ready.
Breakfast:	Have breakfast if possible, or you may have it at school depending on the practice of your school district.

Summer School:	At this time, you'll be on your way to summer school, either catching a bus or being driven to school. During this time, you should prepare yourself mentally to learn something new in your classes. Decide again today that you are going to be the best that you can be as a student, as a classmate, and as a citizen. If you do not have summer school in your district, you can visit any local or public library before noon.
Going Home:	The time to go home from summer school may vary according school districts. Some end summer school at mid day. Some take lunch at school while some do not. If you do not take lunch at school, take your lunch immediately you get home.

Take some Rest:	Free time to relax and to get prepared to do your chores. You can relax for about one hour. During this one hour, you can watch television, or use the computer or just relax on the couch doing nothing.
Do your Chores:	Do your house chores. You have more time during the holidays to carry out your domestic responsibilities. These are tasks that you do with love as a valuable member of your family: it may be dusting the furniture, taking out the trash, washing some dishes, picking up toys, running an errand to the store, feeding the pets, etc.

Do some Readings:	As already indicated, summer vacation is not a time to close all books. You can read novels; books that will make you develop more interests in your dream career, newspapers, and other readings in preparation for your next grade or class
Do your Hobbies:	Summer Vacation is a good opportunity to spend more time on your hobbies. You can spend to thirty minutes to one hour daily on your hobbies.
Physical Activities or Games:	Towards evening when the heat of the sun is not so hard, spend some time with your friends on some physical activities at the play ground to keep fit. You can spend up to one hour before going home to help your parents prepare dinner and to do some

CAJETAN NGOZIKA IHEWULEZI

Family Dinner:	Help your parents to prepare the meals if possible or to set the table for meal. Gather around the table, and after thanking God for that delicious meal, eat and enjoy listening to everyone's stories of the day, and telling one or two of your own.
Family Relaxation:	After family dinner, relax and enjoy doing something you really like: watch a little TV with other family members, practice your talent (drawing, playing a musical instrument,

Bed Time:	Make sure you go to bed on time. To stay awake after 9:30 or ten p.m. during the holidays may be going to bed late. Take a quick shower. Prepare your clothing for the next day's summer school. Get your book bag ready. Bid the whole family good night. Receive your parents' blessings with veneration. Say your prayer of thanks, (prayer before going to sleep).

Prayer of a Latino American Youth for Family Discipline and Peace

Dear God, thank you for making me a member of my family. Thank you for the gift of my parents, my brothers, and sisters. Thank you also for some of our family friends who share our life.

Help me to be a good child by being obedient to my parents and by observing the rules they have made to maintain peace and order in our home. Help me also to learn from my parents the discipline I may need for my suc-

cess in life. Help me to do my chores, my home-work, and other home activities well without complain. Give my parents good health, long life, and the resources to keep taking care of us. Also, give me and my brothers and sisters good health.

When I offend my parents and my siblings, give me the humility to say sorry and to prom-ise not to be bad again. When they offend me, give me the forgiving heart to forgive and to keep loving them. When I am greedy and self-ish, help me to be considerate and to share with others. May your Spirit of love and peace keep dwelling in our family. Amen.

Homework and Questions.

- Do you love and respect your parents? If you do, write out on a sheet of paper three things you can do to show your parents that you love them. After writing them out, show them to your parents

- Do you love and respect your siblings? If you do, write out two things you can do to show them that you love them.

- Is your house always clean or dirty? If it is always dirty, why? Write out four things you can do to make your house clean.

- If you become a professional in future, will your office be dirty or clean? What can you do now in your home to show that in future you can keep your office clean?

- Can you describe yourself as a clean child or a dirty child? If you are always dirty, why? How can you make yourself clean?

- If you become a professional in future, will you like to be a dirty one? If you are a dirty professional, what will happen to your career?

- Do you like doing your studies and homework after school? If you do not like doing your studies, why?

- How many hours do you spend on your studies and homework after school?

- If you do not do your studies or spend enough time on your studies what will happen to your dream career?

- How many hours are you supposed to spend on your studies everyday after school?

- Do you love watching television more than doing your studies? If you spend more time watching television and forget your studies and home work, what will happen to your education and dream career?

CHAPTER THREE

GOING TO SCHOOL AND YOUR DREAM CAREER

My beloved children, you cannot be a professional without going to school and being serious with your education. Being a medical doctor, an attorney or an engineer, for instance, is not just saying what you want to be and being called "little doctor," or "little lawyer," or "little engineer," but it involves really being ready to work hard, especially in those lessons that will help you to qualify for the type of profession you are dreaming about.

There should be respect for one another inside the school bus while on the way to school.

Discipline inside the School Bus

The discipline of going to school starts from what happens inside the school bus. The school bus is out there every morning to take you and your friends or peers to school and to take you back to your home after school. You must be at the bus stop on time in order not to miss the school bus. The journey inside the school bus from your home to school and back should be a journey of peace and respect for one another. You are not expected to pick on one another or hit or step on each other. You are not supposed to use curse words and call each other bad names.

I have already told you what you should do when someone offends you inside the school bus.

1. Do not fight, but report to the bus driver.

2. If the bus driver does not help you, report to your teacher or to the principal.

3. If the teacher or the principal does not help you,

4. Report to your parents, especially if the person keeps bothering you.

In most cases, before you take one or two of these steps, your problem will be solved. On no account should you take laws into your hands and start fighting. Allow reasonable adults who do not take sides to handle such conflicts between you and your schoolmates.

Getting to the School Building

As soon as you get out of the school bus, you go into the school facility. The school facility, whether grade school, high school, or college, should be a peaceful environment where discipline that encourages learning should be highly observed.

The school is made up of the principal, the teachers, other members of the staff, students, including you. When you come to school and see your friends or your classmates, you understand that every child wants to be important and useful in future. Going to school is not a punishment. It is an opportunity for every child who wants to be successful in life and should be taken seriously.

This is a beautiful house of learning. The presence of your friends in this beautiful house shows that education is not a punishment but an opportunity, which every child who wants to be successful in life should be happy to make use of.

The Relationship between You and the School Staff

The principal and the other members of the staff are there to help you to learn. You are supposed to respect, listen, and obey them just as you should respect and obey your parents. As I told you before, you cannot be a professional if you do not know how to follow directions of your leaders. Just as your parents are the leaders in your home, teachers are your leaders in the school. You are like their children and the teachers are like your parents in the school.

Teachers are also supposed to respect and love you. It is their responsibility to help you learn. No good teacher should hate you for any reason. No good teacher who sees you doing your homework well and listening in class should hate you for any reason. They are there to protect you and assist you to build confidence with them and in yourself.

If you are hurt in any way by your schoolmates or by anything else that you cannot handle according to the school rules, your teacher is the first person you should report to. If your teacher does not handle it well, you can report to your principal or the school counselor. If they cannot help you, report to your parents.

You must love and respect your teachers as you love and respect your parents at home. This is one of the keys to your success.

Relationship between You and Your Classmates

The relationship between you and your schoolmates or classmates should also be positive. A future professional should know how to relate to other people. If you cannot relate well with people as a professional, people will not come to you and give you jobs. When people see you are a troublemaker, your profession has failed. You are supposed to learn from both home and school how to be friendly and nice to people.

Make good friends and new ones as many as you can but do not choose bad friends because they will lead you into trouble and make you bad.

You must also respect your school mates and treat them as you would want them treat you.

Discipline in the School Premises

Your school is a place of learning. The school environment should be peaceful and orderly. Discipline at school also involves keeping some rules to help you to concentrate on your class lessons and minimize distraction. Schools have rules, but sometimes the rules may differ a little, depending on the needs of the school or the place where the school is located. Here are sample rules that can help you.

Some General School rules

- Do not be absent from school unless you are sick or your parents have called the school to explain why you are absent.

- Do not come late to school.

- Do not loiter about or run in the hallways when lessons are going on.

- Do not fight.

- Do not struggle over food at meal time.

- Do unto others what you expect them to do unto you.

- Be nice to classmates and make friends with those who have similar interests with you.

There should be discipline in the school premises. It should be a safe environment where love, respect, tolerance, and learning are observed.

Discipline in the Classroom

The classroom is made up of your teacher, your classmates and you. It is where actual learning takes place. Since the actual learning that will help you to be what you want to be takes place in the classroom, you need to be disciplined and observe the classroom rules. Here are some guiding rules that can help you be a good student and to learn.

Some Class Room Rules

- Respect and obey your teachers.

- Listen and pay attention to your teachers when lesson is going on.

- Do not make noise when lessons are going on.

- Do not cheat in class.

- Do not distract yourself and your classmates.

- Apologize to anyone you offend and forgive anyone who hurts you.

- Do not fight in class or call your classmates bad names.

- Report to your teachers if any of your classmates is hurting you or distracting you and does not want to stop.

There should be no distractions or undisciplined behavior in the classroom. It should also be a safe place where love, respect, tolerance, and learning are strictly observed.

What Do You Do When You Are Failing?

No person likes to fail in life, especially when others are doing well. In your school work, you may find out that you are not getting good grades like your classmates. What do you do? Do you fold your hands and continue to fail or do you do something about it? Of course, you have to do something to improve because without doing something to improve your grades, your dreams may not be achieved.

Ask yourself whether you are spending enough time in your studies. As I have told you, if you are spending less than one hour every day or less than seven or eight hours every week on your studies at home, you need to improve. Ask yourself if you are listening attentively to your teachers in the classroom or are you always distracting yourself?

You may seek the advice of your school counselor and your teacher about your low grades. They can advise you better on what to do. Let your parents know about your low grades in case there is anything they can do at home to encourage you to spend more time on your studies. Do not allow your low grade to discourage you from continuing with your education. Instead, see your failure or low grade as an opportunity to work harder to improve.

Also do not forget that when things are getting difficult for you, you also seek the help of God in prayers.

Why Should You Be Serious with Your Education?

As I have already told you, being serious with your education is the only way you can be a professional or achieve your dream. When you are a professional, you will be respected in society; you will have a good job and be paid well. You will also have the opportunity to live in a good house and in a good neighborhood.

Take a look at this beautiful house below. I know you like it and would like to live in it.

You can also be the owner of this house in the future if you study hard and work hard like the person who presently lives in this house.

This house belongs to a person at one time was your age. As a child, he dreamed of becoming somebody important as you are dreaming of now. He behaved well in his family and respected his parents. He tried his best to obey the family rules. He was serious with his education, did his homework well and had good grades. He did the right thing at the right time. He was also a child of prayer.

He went to college and graduated as a professional. Sometimes he had poor grades and some other difficulties in his school work, but he was not discouraged. He did not stop going to school and trying his best. He worked hard, improved his grades and succeeded.

This house belongs to him. He lives in a good neighborhood where there are good roads, good parks for his children to play, good schools, good hospitals, and better security. You can be like him and own a house like this and many other good things if you do what he did. I know you can also do it whether you are a boy or a girl.

There are many other advantages of taking your education seriously and studying hard to be a professional. In the next book (for teenagers), I will tell you more about those advantages.

As I already told you, apart from your efforts to become what you want to be, you cannot do without God. You must always pray to God for success.

Prayer of African American Youth for Educational Success

Dear God, I thank you for giving me the strength to get up every morning to go to school. Thank you for the wisdom to know the importance of education in my life and in my dream to have a career. Thank you for my parents and my teachers who have done a lot to help me progress in my education. Help me to listen attentively in class so as to pass my tests with high grades.

When I am doing poorly in school, help me to pick courage to work harder so as to improve my grades. May your spirit direct me on what I can do to avoid distractions in my studies and to avoid being a source of distraction to others. Help me to respect and obey the school rules. Help me to obey and to respect my teachers. At the end, Lord, crown my efforts with a big success. Amen.

Homework and Questions

- How many hours do you spend on your studies every day?

- Do you do your school homework well and hand it over on time?

- Are you friendly with your teachers and your classmates?

- Would you like to go to college to achieve your dreams?

- What do you do when your grades are getting poor?

- What is your most difficult subject at school, and what are you doing to improve your grades in it or to make sure that you do not fail it?

- What are the advantages of taking your education seriously?

- Do you pray to God for help, especially when things are getting difficult for you in your education?

ENDNOTES

1 Virgil Elizondo, "A Report on Racism: A Mexican American in the United States," *Concilium,* 1 (1982): 63.
2 Marc Morial, "Parents, Young Black Youth and Higher Learning," In a Speech at the National Urban League's 2006 Annual Conference, also available at www.maximsnews. com, 2.
3 Diane Lindsey Reeves and Nancy Heubeck, *Career Ideas for Kids who like Talking* (New York: Fact on File, Inc. 1998), 1.

BIBLIOGRAPHY

Elizondo, Virgil. "A Report on Racism: A Mexican American in the United States," *Concilium*, 1 (1982): 63.

Lindsey, Diane. Reeves and Nancy Heubeck, *Career Ideas for Kids who like Talking.* New York: Fact on File, Inc. 1998.

listen|imagine|view|experience

AUDIO BOOK DOWNLOAD INCLUDED WITH THIS BOOK!

In your hands you hold a complete digital entertainment package. Besides purchasing the paper version of this book, this book includes a free download of the audio version of this book. Simply use the code listed below when visiting our website. Once downloaded to your computer, you can listen to the book through your computer's speakers, burn it to an audio CD or save the file to your portable music device (such as Apple's popular iPod) and listen on the go!

How to get your free audio book digital download:

1. Visit www.tatepublishing.com and click on the e|LIVE logo on the home page.
2. Enter the following coupon code:
   ddb9-39a9-e067-bf7d-eb06-25c3-21fb-9592
3. Download the audio book from your e|LIVE digital locker and begin enjoying your new digital entertainment package today!